17 stories about being a mother while still a child

#CHILDMOTHERS

CONTENT

A BETTER WORLD FOR GIRLS AND WOMEN

Introduction by Her Royal Highness, Crown Princess Mary of Denmark

When I visited Burkina Faso in April 2016, I met Kiswendsida. She is a lovely young girl, 15 years old and as any other young teenager, with her whole life in front of her. I also met her daughter, Koudbi, a beautiful, one month old baby. Kiswendsida is one of the young mothers we meet in this book.

Kiswendsida is a strong, young mother. Against all odds – and thankfully due to the support from her grandmother – she managed to stay in school during her pregnancy and returned to school already a week after giving birth. Kiswendsida has big dreams, she dreams of becoming an architect.

Still, Kiswendsida thinks it's hard work being a mother. Although she loves her daughter, she wishes she'd known how to avoid becoming pregnant. She says she will wait to have more children and that she believes 26 is probably the right age to become a mother.

The captivating portraits in this book – of Kiswendsida and 16 other young mothers – represent the real-life stories of very young girls, who have become adults before their time. They have become mothers while they were still children. Although each story is unique, they do share many similarities.

These are stories about poverty, ignorance, and lack of opportunities in life. About young love, abuse and coercion. About the serious complications that can occur when a young girl becomes pregnant and gives birth before her body is fully developed.

Becoming a mother should be a happy event – a positive choice of giving life without fearing for your own. But unfortunately, this is not the case in all parts of the world.

In 2009, I attended a Mother's Day celebration, where a female obstetrician from Chad in Central Africa explained that in

HRH The Crown Princess with Kiswensida, 15 years old, and her daughter Khoudbi, one month old. Burkina Faso, 2015.

her country, when a woman gets pregnant she has one foot in the grave. I was shocked to learn that every second minute a woman dies during pregnancy or while giving birth. These alarming facts led to my involvement and desire to contribute to improving conditions for women during pregnancy and childbirth.

The obstetrician was Grace Kodindo. She was in Denmark to present the film, *Dead Mums Don't Cry*, about her work in Chad to save the lives of women and their babies during pregnancy and childbirth. The film documents how inadequate access to basic health services and essential medicines leads to poor women dying from causes that could have been prevented or treated.

My commitment has only grown stronger since then as I have learnt more about the challenges that girls and women face around the world.

SUFFERING THAT NO GIRL SHOULD ENDURE

In 2010, I met two women who had lived with obstetric fistula – an injury that occurs as a result of prolonged and obstructed labour where qualified and timely assistance has not been available. It was my first encounter with women who had suffered this type of birth injury.

Fistula causes incontinence of urine and/or stool. In addition to these health-related consequences, women living with fistula

7

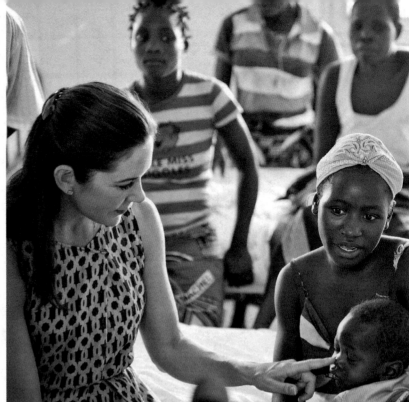

Left: HRH The Crown Princess at the Mother's Day event "The Art of Saving a Mother" with Dr. Grace Kodindo and Danish Minister for Development Cooperation Ulla Tørnæs. The National Gallery. Denmark, 2009. *Right*: HRH The Crown Princess at a fistula hospital with "the miracle baby" who had survived a difficult birth during which the mother developed an obstetric fistula. Mozambique, 2012.

are; often deserted by their husbands, cast out by their community and have to endure miserable lives in isolation and loneliness.

Young pregnant women who are not yet fully developed are at particular risk for obstetric fistula. In this book, we meet Anita from Bangladesh, who is 15 years old. She was in labour for two days before being admitted to hospital. Her child was stillborn, and she suffered a fistula. Compared to many others, Anita was lucky to receive reconstructive surgery for her fistula. Her hopes are to return to a normal life.

During my visit to Mozambique in 2012 and Burkina Faso in 2016, I met women who had undergone fistula surgery in clinics funded by UNFPA, the United Nations Population Fund. The hope in these women's eyes was testimony to the unbearable suffering they've endured and how they dreamt of returning to the lives they once knew.

A LONG STRUGGLE FOR HEALTH AND RIGHTS

2010 was also the year when I became Patron of UNFPA – the UN organisation that works to ensure that; every pregnancy is wanted, every childbirth is safe and that every young person's potential is fulfilled.

Planned pregnancy and safe childbirth are two aspects of the concept, 'sexual and reproductive health and rights', which

HRH The Crown Princess with representatives from the youth organization Coalizâo. The lively discussion and debate gave The Crown Princess insight into and a better understanding of the situation for youth and the use of contraceptives in Mozambique. Mozambique, 2012.

includes the right to decide when to have children, how many to have, with whom, and to have them without risking your life or health in the process. This has been recognised as a human right since 1968.

Central to sexual and reproductive health and rights is; the dissemination of adequate information, access to contraception that protects against unwanted pregnancy and sexually transmitted infections such as hiv/aids and qualified assistance before, during and after childbirth. It also includes efforts to eliminate harmful traditional practices,

such as child marriage and female genital mutilation (FGM) – practices that violate the rights of girls and have a negative impact on their health.

During my visit to Ethiopia and Senegal in 2015, I met young girls who have suffered FGM. They had not only experienced the pain of the procedure, their human rights had also been violated. In cases where FGM causes serious infection or severe blood loss, the harmful practice can be fatal. Some survivors experience chronic pain and complications in connection with childbirth. This is particularly

9

the case if the mother has been subjected to the most severe form of FGM.

One of the girls in this book, Poko, was subjected to FGM when she was a little girl. Poko almost died from blood loss when she gave birth. We cannot be sure that Poko's complications during delivery were caused by her genital cuts but, we know that when communities are informed about the risks associated with FGM, this new knowledge becomes an argument for stopping the practice.

FGM has been mistakenly perceived to be based on religion. However, it is not prescribed by any religion. In fact it is practiced in both Muslim and Christian communities.

HRH The Crown Princess visits a project which works to end female genital mutilation and child marriage in the Afambo district. Ethiopia, 2015.

That's why it is so important to engage local imams and priests in the work to eliminate FGM.

Increased awareness and knowledge pave the way for real and lasting change. Parents want the best for their children. And with increased awareness, parents can change their beliefs on how to best ensure the acceptance, respect and security of their daughters.

To put an end to these practices, the entire community must be involved. Only when a critical mass agrees to end a social norm, can a new understanding of what is best for girls become a reality.

Ending female genital mutilation and child marriage requires a long-term focus and an continuous effort. The local community needs to truly understand the harmful consequences and see the value of giving girls and women other opportunities in life – on equal footing with boys and men. This means, for example; allowing them to continue their education, inherit, own their own land, and have their own bank account.

MEN ARE PART OF THE SOLUTION

Several of the young girls we meet in this book find themselves in situations that arise out of inequality between women and men, girls and boys. Aïssa from Burkina Faso who shares her story with us in this book,

has been a victim of gender-based violence. Gender based violence is an extreme expression of inequality, which affects one in three women in the world.

Nonetheless, it is clear that men and boys are part of the solution. In South Africa and Burkina Faso, I have met men who play a key role in improving the lives of women and girls.

During my visit to South Africa in 2014, I spoke with men who previously had been violent offenders against women. Now they work to change the attitudes of other men in their communities.

In Burkina Faso, I visited the so-called "husband schools" – an initiative developed with the support of UNFPA and one that is now present in several other countries. At these schools, married men get information about women's reproductive health. For example, they learn about the importance of spacing pregnancies, of regular examinations during pregnancy, and of giving birth with the assistance of a qualified midwife. Through the involvement of men, women are supported and more likely to access available health care services.

ESSENTIAL INFORMATION

I have seen many examples of programmes that work and globally, we are making good progress. We have witnessed; a strong increase in the number of girls, who now

HRH The Crown Princess greets men who are involved in the husband's school in the village of Kamse. Burkina Faso, 2016.

finish primary school, an increasing number of communities have stopped the practice of FGM and today, most countries have legislation in place to protect girls from harmful traditions such as FGM and child marriage.

These are important steps. But if girls like the ones in this book are to have an alternative choice, then we must protect and respect their basic human rights and the vision of letting young people decide for themselves when to have children.

It will take a collective effort to break what is perhaps the most widespread taboo of all – comprehensive sexuality education. Young people need to be knowledgeable about; puberty, why their body is changing, how children are conceived and how to protect yourself from unwanted pregnancy.

Research shows that when young people receive accurate, age-relevant sex education and have access to contraception, they are better at protecting themselves.

However, this remains a controversial issue. Today, only a minority of young people in developing countries have adequate knowledge of, or access to contraception.

It's not just a question of factual knowledge, it's also about building self-esteem – especially for young girls. They have to be confident and in a position to be able to make decisions about their own bodies. That it's their decision and right to say 'no'. Similarly, boys need to respect that 'no' means 'no' and understand that they are no-less of a man when they respect girls and women – actually, it is the contrary.

HRH The Crown Princess has taken this photo at a meeting with locals who shared their concerns in maintaining a sustainable livelihood in the face of climate change, drought and poverty, without the means to plan their families. Ethiopia, 2005.

IMPRESSIVE STRENGTH

In my view, increased equality between women and men, girls and boys is a catalyst for positive change. And I believe this is confirmed by the stories in this important book. All these girls have great potential, and with everything they have already endured in their lives, they have already demonstrated impressive resilience and strength.

The three young girls from Syria – Amira, Muna and Zainab – are admirable examples of this. They have not only managed motherhood at a very young age, they've done so as refugees. Humanitarian crises undermine

the lives of everyone but, for pregnant women the situation is even more acute. Tragically, we see examples of women refugees giving birth, literally on the side of the road.

In 2013, I visited one of the world's largest refugee camps, the Zaatari camp in Jordan, where UNFPA has established a maternity clinic. Here, in fairly simple facilities, qualified staff are ready to assist women when they give birth. Such clinics save lives. Since the camp was established in June 2012, more than 7,000 children have been born at the clinic – and no mother has died giving birth.

Becoming a mother is not just about sur-viving and coping with the delivery, although a couple of the girls in this book have been frightfully close to dying. Very often, the opportunities for young mothers' in life become limited. Pregnancy often means that they are unable to continue or finish their education and given that education is often the key to breaking the cycle of poverty, they end up perpetuating it and passing it on to their own children.

This vicious cycle must be broken. However, to achieve this we must view development issues in a larger context.

COMMON GOALS FOR A BETTER WORLD

In 2015, the countries of the world adopted *The Sustainable Developments Goals* – 17 new goals for global development. Two of these goals are health and gender equality related. Among the specific targets for these two goals are; putting an end to FGM and child marriage, reducing maternal mortality and ensuring universal access to sexual and reproductive health services.

The ambition is to fulfil the 17 development goals by 2030. In other words, the interna-tional community has committed to a short and clearly defined time frame of 15 years to bring about substantial improvements for the planet and its people. To reach these goals it will require a significant and concerted effort from everyone – citizens, local com-munities, the private sector, governments and leaders in all countries. If we *do* suc-ceed, the girls we meet in this book will see their children grow up in a rapidly changing world. They will experience that their chil-dren will have better opportunities as teen-agers than what they have had.

In 2012, I had the privilege of becoming a member of the High-Level Task Force on ICPD, the International Conference on Population and Development, working with some of the world's leading authorities and advocates in this field. The task force has worked to ensure that present and future generations of children and young people are able to choose the life they want – without being overtaken prematurely by adulthood, as the girls in this book have been.

FROM DREAM TO OPPORTUNITY

Like every parent, these girls want the best for their children. Some have already given up on their own dreams of getting an edu-cation and a job – and are now hoping that their children will have the opportunities they had to abandon.

In engaging with women and girls around the world there are two things that strike me. On the one hand, how disturbing it is that we continue to witness abuse and violation of women's basic human rights

HRH The Crown Princess visits the Zaatari refugee camp which hosts refugees from Syria. Jordan, 2013.

and on the other hand, how very encouraging it is that in every community I visit, I meet amazing women with huge potential to make positive change – if they only get the chance. These women give me hope for the future.

We must give the girls and boys of the world the opportunity to contribute to making progress – in their family, in their local community, in their country, in the world. We need to make sure girls and women have a better chance of realising their potential. Everyone will benefit if we do. And we need to involve boys and men in the effort to achieving greater gender equality.

The girls in this book have dreams of a better life, a better future – for themselves and especially for their children. We must make it possible for them to turn their dreams into a reality.

CHAPTER 1
WHEN GIRLS BECOME MOTHERS

E very day, thousands of girls who have not yet turned 15 give birth. They move directly from childhood to motherhood – with the responsibility and obligations that this entails.

The majority of these very young mothers are already married. Many do not attend school, and most of them face a future with many children and domestic responsibilities.

When young girls get married, they often feel social pressure to have children in order to prove their fertility. Still, a large proportion of pregnancies among adolescent girls are unintended – simply because these young girls don't have sufficient knowledge about their bodies; they don't know how to have children or how to prevent it.

Young girls under 15, who do not have access to a well-functioning health system, are at a greater risk of experiencing complications during pregnancy and childbirth. The complications can cause permanent injury or, in worst cases, be life threatening for the young mother and her child. Every year, tens of thousands of young girls die due to complications in connection with pregnancy, unsafe abortion or childbirth. Their children are also at a significant higher risk of dying during birth or before their first birthday, than children born by adult women.

During the teenage years adolescents should be enabled to make the important life choices that they will face on their way to adulthood: which education or vocational training they want; who they wish to spend their life with; and last but not least when – or if – they wish to marry and start a family.

IT IS LONELY TO BE A MOTHER

KISWENDSIDA (15), THE MOTHER OF KOUDBI, ONE MONTH OLD, BURKINA FASO

Kiswendsida lives with her daughter, her grandparents and her aunts in the outskirts of an urban area in Burkina Faso. Her parents work in the Ivory Coast. Kiswendsida had very limited sexuality education in school and got pregnant at the age of 14. She was able to continue school thanks to support from her grandmother.

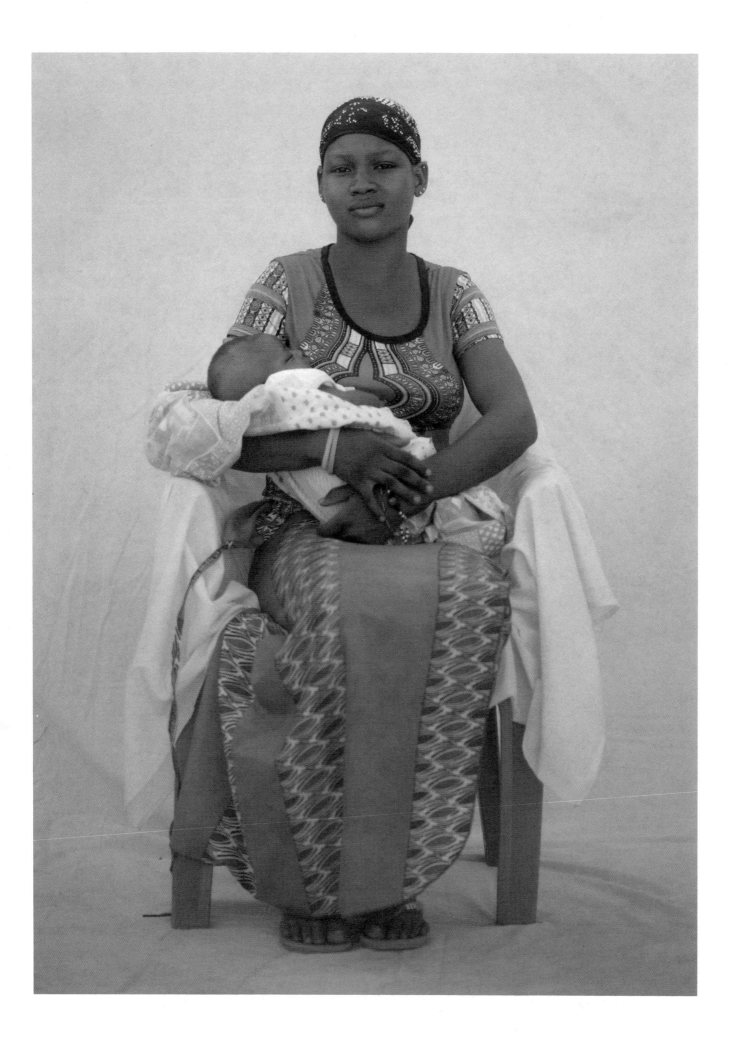

While I was pregnant I continued going to school. One week after I gave birth I was back in class. I didn't want to abandon my studies.

Kiswendsida 15 years old

KISWENSIDAS STORY

I got pregnant at fourteen. I had a boyfriend who lives nearby. When I realized I was pregnant I told him. We could talk about it but now I don't see him anymore. My family reacted badly when they found out. My pregnancy and delivery went well – no problems.

While I was pregnant I continued going to school. The other students were not mean, they were very supportive. I did not know anything about contraception; we did not learn about it in school. One week after I gave birth I was back in class. I didn't want to abandon my studies. My grandmother has supported me all this time and she is the one who helps me take care of the baby so I can go to school.

It's hard to be a mother. I feel alone and miss my parents. They work in the Ivory Coast and haven't seen the baby yet. In the future, I would like to have more children, but not now. I think 26 would be a good age. My dream is to become an architect and I would like my daughter to go to school.

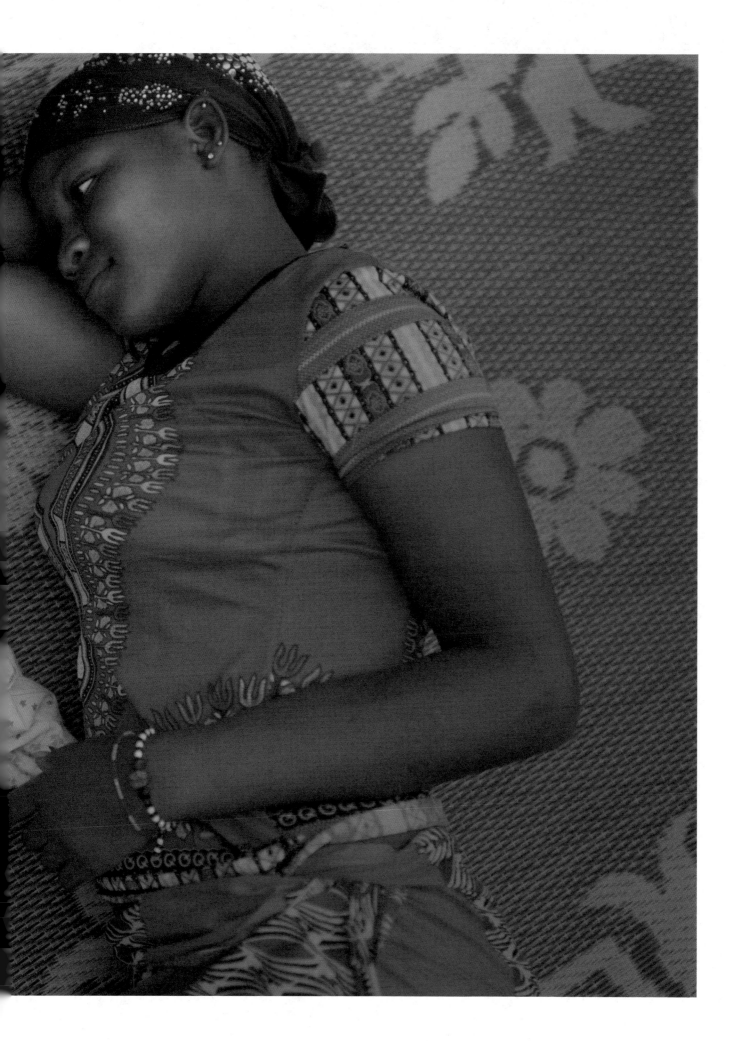

I WILL GIVE MY DAUGHTER EVERYTHING

RABEYA (16), MOTHER OF KUSHUM, THREE YEARS OLD, BANGLADESH

Rabeya got married at 13. She lives with her husband, her three-year old daughter, and her in-laws in a rural area in Bangladesh. During her three pregnancies, she lost a lot of weight and suffered from anaemia. Only one of her children has survived. Rabeya has now agreed with her husband that they should use contraception and have no more children.

RABEYA'S STORY

I'm very happy to be Kushum's mother. I like when she's sleeping safely in my lap. She sleeps with me all the time; if she doesn't, I feel empty. It was hard when she was a baby. Then I had to feed her and keep her in my arms all the time. Now everyone takes care of her and plays with her. She's the only child in the family so everyone adores her.

I didn't realize when I got pregnant the first time at 13. I threw up and often felt sick. Then the others told me that I was pregnant. I became very thin - like a stick. So even though the size of my belly grew, I was losing weight. I even used to faint while I was cooking.

I had no knowledge about sexual education or family planning. I didn't have any interest in learning about that. My mother and sister explained it to me but I cannot talk about these things to my husband.

Actually, since I was 13, I have been pregnant three times. Kushum is my first daughter and the only one who survived. When she just started walking, I got pregnant again but the baby died inside me. Then last year, I had a third daughter but she was born with a severe illness and died when she was only three months old.

After I lost my baby last year, my aunt told me to go to the local health centre and get contraceptive injections. Since then I haven't had a period. I feel much better and I'm gaining weight. Now, I don't want to have any more children. I don't have any more energy. I'm happy with my one child and thankfully my husband agrees.

Now, after three years, I understand a little more about marriage. Marriage is a combination of good and bad. My husband is a very nice man. Before I was married I dreamed of becoming a teacher. As I'm married now and have a family, nobody is going to support that. I have to manage my own household. My dream, though, is that my child, my husband and I buy our own house where we're happy. For Kushum, I dream big. I want her to know, that when she grows up she can do anything she wants. I want to give her everything.

Before I was married I dreamed of becoming a teacher. As I'm married now and have a family, nobody is going to support that.

Rabeya 16 years old

Since I was 13, I have been pregnant three times. Kushum is my first daughter and the only one who survived. When she just started walking, I got pregnant again but the baby died inside me. Then last year, I had a third daughter but she was born with a severe illness and died when she was only three months old. Now, I don't want to have any more children.

Rabeya 16 years old

I MISS SCHOOL AND FRIENDS

ANGELICA (13), MOTHER OF LUCNER, THREE MONTHS OLD, HAITI

Angelica lives with her parents, her siblings and her son in a violent urban slum area in Haiti. She met her boyfriend, became pregnant and had to leave school when she was in seventh grade. Her boyfriend continues school like before.

ANGELICA'S STORY

I knew there was a risk of getting pregnant. But I didn't think it would happen to me. In school we didn't learn much about these things. I have a boyfriend who is 16 and we have been a couple for a while. When I got pregnant, my father kicked me out of the house. I had to sleep on people's doorsteps. Once in a while my mother would send me food. I shouldn't have had a baby at my age. I'm too young. I can't even take care of him.

I live with my parents and eight siblings in a poor area of the city. We lost our house in the earthquake. My mother is the only one earning our living. Her business isn't doing well and she's always borrowing money. She's my only friend. She's always supporting me, even though I've let her down.

When I was pregnant, I got extremely skinny because I wasn't getting enough food. It was hard; I wasn't in school and had to sleep on the streets.

When I went into labour, my mum was out. I went to several clinics, but they couldn't help me because my case was too severe. There was a high risk that both the baby and I would die. I remember that they also didn't let me in at the maternity clinic because I didn't have any money. I was lying on the pavement outside in the worst pain. Then a woman came by and helped me, lending me money for medication and a C-section.

When I came back from the hospital with the baby, my father first refused to let me inside. He said he couldn't be responsible for a daughter with a child. Our neighbours helped me. They gave me a place to sleep with my baby, some food and something to drink.

Only recently was I allowed to come back home – and now I have to take care of everything. I have to wake up early in the morning to go and fetch water. I come back and cook for my younger siblings and take them to school. Then I do the laundry. I don't always get enough food for myself and also do not have enough for my baby.

My dream is to go back to school; I liked it so much. We were a group of friends who would perform and sing. It's sad to see my friends going to school without me. Even my boyfriend continues to go to school like before, while I need to stay at home. My one wish is that my son will get an education.

My advice to other girls is that if they decide to have a boyfriend, they should get informed and use contraception so that they don't become pregnant like I did at such a young age.

I shouldn't have had a baby at my age. I'm too young. I can't even take care of him. My dream is to go back to school; I liked it so much. We were a group of friends who would perform and sing. It's sad to see my friends going to school without me. Even my boyfriend continues to go to school like before, while I need to stay at home.

Angelica 13 years old

NOW MY LIFE IS ALL ABOUT MY CHILDREN

ZAINAB (15), MOTHER OF BILAL, TWO YEARS OLD, AND
KARIMA, EIGHT MONTHS OLD, JORDAN

Zainab lives with her husband and their two children in a refugee
camp in Jordan. She has left school and has no desire to finish
her education. Zainab knows where she can get advice on family
planning, but she worries about the side effects of contraception.

Before, I didn't know anything about these things, but now I'd like to use contraception. It's easy to get here but I haven't done it yet. I've heard that some of them have side effects. I was told that the contraception I wanted causes headaches, so I got scared.

Zainab 15 years old

ZAINAB'S STORY

My husband and I were in love before we got married in 2013.
We dated first. He's 12 years older than me and works with olives.

I used to go to school in my home country Syria, but we had
to flee because of the war. Now we live in a refugee camp. I take
care of my children and husband, cook, clean and fetch water.
When he comes home from work, I heat up water for him to take
a bath.

I was so happy when I got pregnant at 13. I had no complications during my pregnancy, thank God. When my husband and
I had problems, we got help from an organization that taught us
more about being married and what it's like to be a mother.

Before, I didn't know anything about these things, but now
I'd like to use contraception. It's easy to get here but I haven't
done it yet. I've heard that some of them have side effects. I was
told that the contraception I wanted causes headaches, so I got
scared.

I gave birth here in a camp clinic without any problems. It's a
bit difficult to be a mother, but my children always entertain me.
I'm happy. I'm always happy.

My life now is all about my children. I don't want to go back
to school. I have a responsibility to take care of my children, my
husband and my home. That's it. Before, I wanted to be a nurse.
But now, this is my future – to take care of my children and raise
them. I want them to have a happy future and a happy life.

I WONDER WHY I HAD MY BABY

TAONGA (15), MOTHER OF MARGARET, FOUR MONTHS OLD, ZAMBIA

Taonga lives with her daughter, aunt and cousins in a very remote area in Zambia. She stopped attending school during her pregnancy and doesn't know if she will be able to go back again since her family has no money.

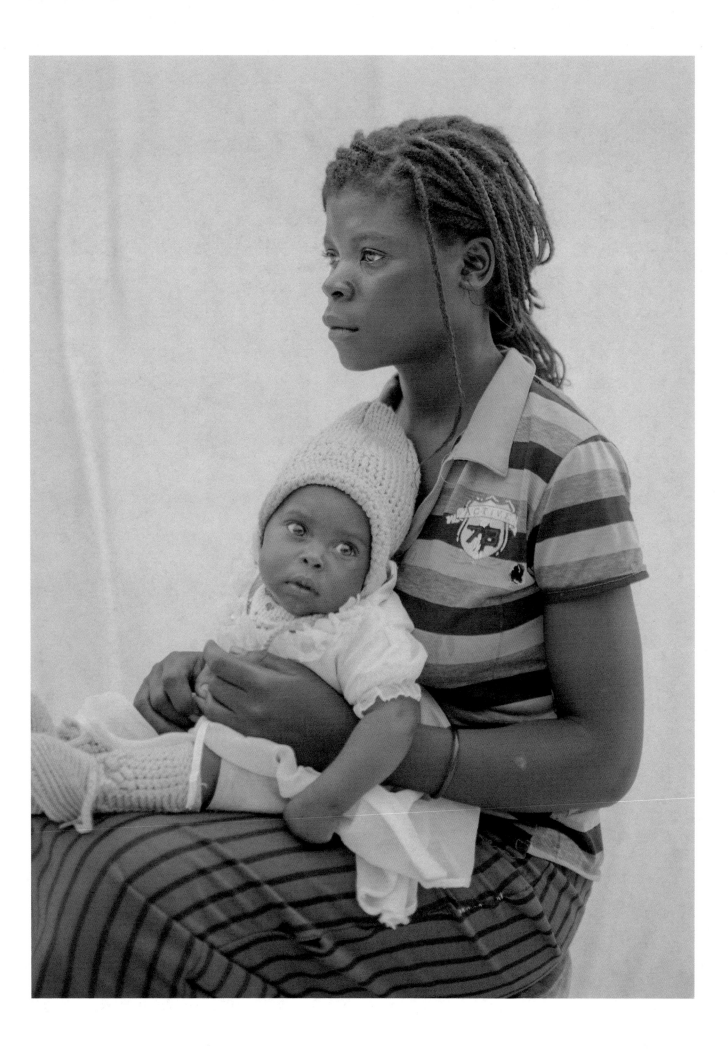

TAONGA'S STORY

I met Margaret's father in school. He's older than me. He used to live nearby but now he has moved to another town. He came to visit when Margaret was born but now there is no communication between us. I don't have a phone and he doesn't come to see us.

In school we only learned about periods. I didn't think I would get pregnant. I'd heard that you can have injections, though, to prevent pregnancy.

I'm feeling good, but I wonder why I had my baby. It's not easy for me. I enjoy looking at her but not the responsibility of taking care of a child. My aunt helps me out but my baby cries a lot. And because she is still breastfeeding, I always need to be close by.

I wish I could go back to school or get married so that I can provide well for my child in the future. I would love to be a teacher or a community worker. I wish that one day Margaret will be able to go to school.

MABLE PHIRI IS TAONGA'S AUNT, WHOM SHE HAS LIVED WITH SINCE SHE WAS FIVE. MABLE PHIRI'S ACCOUNT:

Taonga is very sad to have the baby. It has also been additional work for me. I've my own children to take care of. The father of Margaret once lived around here. He came here but Taonga refused to see him. Then he came again. Taonga says they only had sex three times. One day I noticed that her belly was getting bigger and that's when I took her to the health clinic to take a pregnancy test. We went to the father's house and told him that he should pay for it. He never paid. Instead he moved somewhere else.

I'm feeling good, but I wonder why I had my baby. It's not easy for me. I enjoy looking at her but not the responsibility of taking care of a child. My aunt helps me out but my baby cries a lot. And because she is still breastfeeding, I always need to be close by.

Taonga 15 years old

I wish I could go back to school or get married so that I can provide well for my child in the future.

Taonga 15 years old

CHAPTER 2
A CHILD AND ALREADY A BRIDE

C hild marriage and motherhood in childhood are closely related since nine out of ten child mothers are already married. After her wedding, a girl will often be expected to prove her fertility.

Despite child marriage being prohibited by international law and by national laws in many countries, one in nine girls in developing countries* is married before they turn 15. And one in three is married before they turn 18 (*except China).

Marrying off daughters at an early age can be part of the local culture – or simply caused by poverty. Cultural, economic or humanitarian circumstances may explain why parents see marriage as a way of protecting their daughter, safeguarding her honour, or giving her better opportunities in life – for instance by getting her out of a refugee camp.

Whatever the reason, child marriage is a violation of human rights and is defined in international agreements as a harmful traditional practice. As girls are often married off to much older men, child marriage also represents an extreme form of gender inequality. For the young girl, early marriage often means the end of her schooling and the prospect of a life in poverty.

While boys are also married as children, child marriages affect girls in much greater numbers.

The practice of child marriage can be ended when the local community truly understands the harmful consequences and see the value of giving girls and women other opportunities in life.

HRH Crown Princess Mary

YOU CHANGE WHEN YOU MARRY

NARGIS (15), MOTHER OF NAYEEM, 1 1/2 YEAR OLD, BANGLADESH

Nargis lives with her husband, son and her in-laws in a rural village in Bangladesh. Her parents did not want her to marry. But they say they had no choice since they could not afford to support her anymore. Nargis works in a garment factory to save money for her son's future education.

NARGIS' STORY

I studied until the eighth grade. I really liked school; my favourite subject was science. I had a dream to study law, but my parents couldn't afford it.

Although I knew of the consequences of an early marriage, I still ended up getting married at 14 because my parents are extremely poor. At the time of the wedding, I was very nervous. I didn't know my husband and even now I don't know his age - I think he's around 25. He works in sales. I didn't want to move into his house. I remember crying a lot. Everyone around me somehow convinced me, though.

I didn't know anything about the body. I started having my periods only two or three months before my marriage. I got pregnant and I was fine, I didn't feel sick. At first I didn't want to be a mother but after getting married, people change their mind. You don't think like before.

I had some complications during my labour so I was supposed to have a C-section. However, due to my very low blood count, they couldn't do it. I had a normal delivery instead and it was very painful. I wasn't afraid, but it was so hard.

I felt happy seeing my son for the first time. I didn't recognise this feeling before and now I understand how it feels to be a mother. My husband was also very happy. He always wanted a son. Now I take contraceptive pills. It was my husband who suggested this idea. I don't want any more children right now.

I'm working in a garment factory to save enough money for the future so that my son can get an education and move forward in life. I stitch sleeves. It's not so hard; the machine does all the work.

I get up at 5:30 in the morning and cook breakfast. Then I have a shower and feed my son. At seven o'clock I leave Nayeem with my mother and take the staff bus. I get back from work around eight o'clock in the evening. If my son is sleeping, I don't wake him up. If he's awake I feed him and get him ready for bed. I feel bad that I'm away from him all day. But when he starts school I won't work anymore. Then I'll be there to help him with his studies.

For now, all my future plans are for my son. When he turns three, he'll start school. I do have dreams of my own and that's to pass my exams and finish school. My husband has said that he will let me study later. I'm happy with my life. I'm married and I have a son. Do people ever stay the same after this?

Although I knew of the consequences of an early marriage, I still ended up getting married at 14 because my parents are extremely poor. At first I didn't want to be a mother but after getting married, people change their mind. You don't think like before.

Nargis 15 years old

MY PARENTS FORCED ME TO MARRY

THANDIWE (15), MOTHER OF ANNA, NINE MONTHS OLD, ZAMBIA

Thandiwe lives with her daughter, her husband and her in-laws in a remote village in Zambia. When Thandiwe was pregnant, she had to leave school and she was forced to marry the father of her child.

THANDIWE'S STORY

I still don't feel ready to be a mother. I had never thought to have a child now. When I got pregnant, I was in the sixth grade. I wanted to become a chef and work in town. Then I met a boy who was in the ninth grade. We didn't have a relationship, we only met about five times – that's all. I was scared when I found out I was pregnant. When my parents knew about it, they brought me to my husband's house and just left me. I didn't want to marry him, but they forced me.

During the pregnancy, I was here with my husband and we planted crops in the fields. When my labour pains started, I was taken to the clinic with money given by my parents. The delivery was very difficult; it took two days. I ruptured my vagina, got stitches and was given salt water to apply as treatment. I was told to come to the clinic after one month to get an injectable contraceptive. So I did. Right now I don't want any more children; maybe when Anna gets older.

I have no time to myself. When I wake up at four o'clock in the morning I sweep the yard, wash plates, collect water, look for firewood, cook and wash clothes. Then my husband and I go to the fields to work. We come back around two o'clock in the afternoon. In the meantime, Anna stays with her grandmother. She is the one who helps me most. She looks after Anna, helps with washing the clothes and buys me soap.

I haven't visited my family since I came back from the clinic after my delivery. My husband and in-laws don't allow me to make many visits to my family. My parents come sometimes, though, and bring along things for Anna.

When I think about the future I only think about my education. I liked math and would love to go back to school. I've talked with my husband about this and he said I could go back to school after

Anna grows up and is able to walk. I don't have any set plans for Anna but I do hope she will get an education. When she gets older I will tell her, "My child, work hard and finish your education. Don't rush into marriage. Finish your schooling so that you can support us as well in the future".

I was scared when I found out I was pregnant. When my parents knew about it, they brought me to my husband's house and just left me. I didn't want to marry him, but they forced me.

Thandiwe 15 years old

CHAPTER 3
YOU DON'T CUT A GIRL

Female genital mutilation (FGM) is a violation of human rights. The painful procedure is most often performed without anaesthetics, and the same knife is used for several girls without sterilisation between cuts. In case of excessive bleeding or infection, the procedure can be fatal. It can also cause chronic pain, for instance when urinating.

FGM refers to a range of procedures involving the partial or total removal of the external female genitalia. It is estimated that thousands of girls are subjected to FGM every day – and that around 200 million women and girls worldwide live with the consequences of these procedures.

Women who have been subjected to the most severe form of FGM – leaving them with only a small opening – are more likely to experience complications during labour and have a greater risk of giving birth to a stillborn baby.

In the local communities where FGM is practiced, it's seen as a precondition for earning respect and acceptance – and for being eligible for marriage. However, it's often considered taboo to discuss FGM. For this reason, many parents do not question the tradition but consider it a precondition to ensure their daughter a good life.

There is international agreement that FGM is a harmful traditional practice, and it's banned in most countries. FGM is primarily practiced in countries in the northern half of the African continent, but also in the Middle East, Asia and Latin America. The tradition is found in Christian, Muslim and other religious societies, but not prescribed by any of these religions.

I WAS BETWEEN LIFE AND DEATH

POKO (15), MOTHER OF TIGA, THREE YEARS OLD,
BURKINA FASO

Poko lives with her son, her parents, her grandmother
and her aunt in an urban area in Burkina Faso. After
being subjected to female genital mutilation (FGM)
at age four, she got pregnant when she was twelve
years old and almost died during childbirth. Poko's
family is very poor and cannot pay the school fees
for Poko to continue her education.

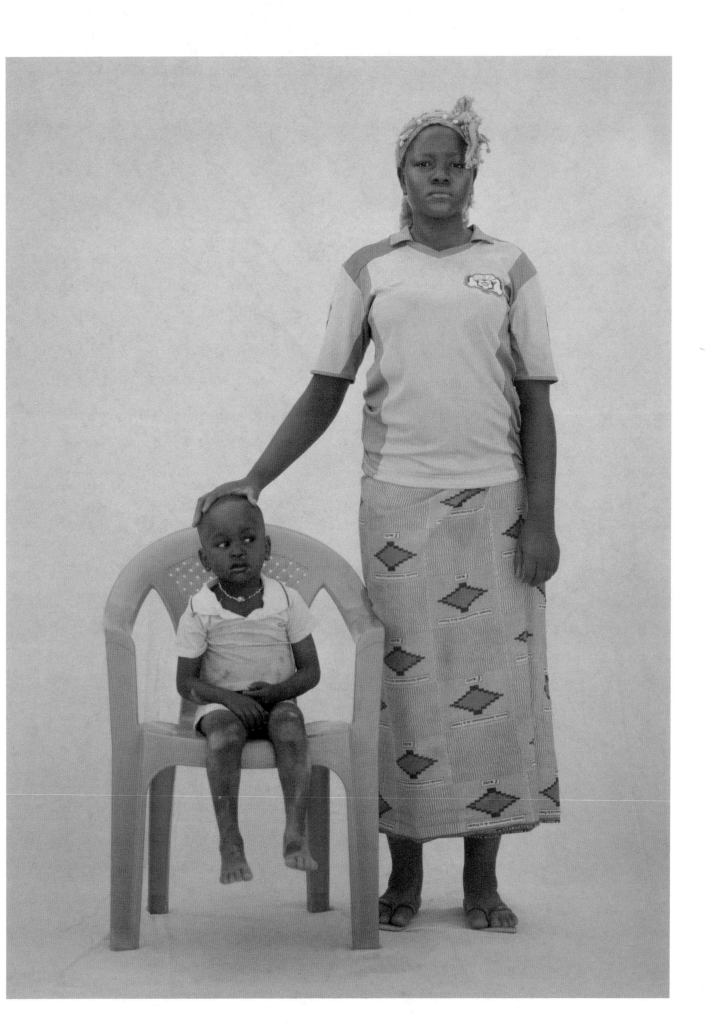

I was cut, when I
was four years old.
I do not remember
it. But in my family
we do not cut the
girls anymore.

Poko 15 years old

For the delivery, I was supposed to have a caesarean section, but it was too expensive.

Poko 15 years old

POKO'S STORY

I was cut, when I was four years old. I do not remember it. But in my family we do not cut the girls anymore.

I was twelve when I got pregnant. I didn't know anything about these things. One day, a guy I used to meet wanted me to come to his place. I did not know why, but he said that when the night came, we could sleep together. I went there and he made love to me. It was my first time.

At first, I didn't realize that I was pregnant. It was my older sister who told me. She noticed that my stomach had grown big. I got a bit embarrassed and even cried. My sister kept the secret for six months before telling my parents. For the delivery, I was supposed to have a caesarean section, but it was too expensive. At the hospital, they said I was too young and sent me off to a local health clinic.

I lost a lot of blood during labour, but since we had no money, we couldn't pay for blood transfusions. So I came back home, used traditional medicine and was in bed for two months after the delivery. I was in between life and death. I do not know if I lost so much blood because I was cut as a child.

I don't see the father of my son. When I got pregnant, he refused to accept responsibility of the baby. Life as a mother is difficult. We don't have enough to eat; we don't have food every day, or any soap to wash our clothes. I used to go to school but now I'm just at home. I take care of my son and help my mother selling moringa leaves. I'd like to go back to school.

CHAPTER 4
THE BIRDS AND THE BEES

Adolescents should have comprehensive sexuality education and access to contraception. Research shows that if they have basic information about how their bodies develop; how to conceive children; and how to avoid getting pregnant, their sexual debut will be delayed – and they will adopt safer sexual practices.

Sex education can be provided in or outside of school – for instance by teachers, community health workers, youth workers, or peer educators. Access to contraception can be provided at youth centres or local health clinics – in a friendly and non-judgemental atmosphere.

It's important that the initiatives targeted at young people also serve to build self-esteem, decision-making skills, and the ability to resist peer pressure.

Although the advantages of sex education are well documented, the majority of young people in developing countries enter puberty without having the necessary knowledge or access to contraception. In most of Africa and in parts of Asia, less than half of young girls who wish to prevent pregnancy use contraception. This puts them at high risk of an unwanted pregnancy.

There are many reasons why young people do not use contraception. They may fear being condemned in their community; they might not be able to afford it; or they may not have sufficient information about contraception, let alone know where to get hold of it or how to use it. Gender inequality can also make it difficult for girls to insist on condom use.

If girls like the ones in this book are to have an alternative choice, then we must protect and respect their basic human rights and the vision of letting young people decide for themselves when to have children.

HRH Crown Princess Mary

WE DID NOT LEARN ABOUT THOSE THINGS IN SCHOOL

MULENGA (14), MOTHER OF FELICITY, FIVE WEEKS OLD, ZAMBIA

Mulenga lives with her daughter, her parents, her father's second wife and her ten siblings in a remote village in Zambia. She used to go to school and wanted to become a doctor when her mother discovered Mulenga was pregnant. She had not had sexuality education in school and did not know that you risk pregnancy, when you have sex. Mulenga takes her daughter to health checks at the local clinic and gets her vaccinated. At the clinic she meets with other young mothers.

MULENGA'S STORY

It's difficult being a mother. I don't have time to play anymore. My daughter often cries and I have to stay at home and take care of her and wash nappies. Before I had a baby, I used to play and go wherever I wanted. I liked playing football.

I had no idea how you get pregnant. I didn't even know I was pregnant. We didn't learn about those things at school. It was my mother who told me I wasn't looking well. When I realized I was going to have a child, I was upset and annoyed. My mother was too. I told my boyfriend, but he denied responsibility.

My father took me to my boyfriend's home and told his parents: 'We've brought this child here because she's pregnant. You can only return her once you've paid us 5,000 Kwacha.' It took four months before they paid a third of the money and I had to stay there during that time. He's not my boyfriend anymore, but we talk to each other sometimes.

I was afraid of the delivery. When the nurse told me what it was like to give birth, I thought I might die. I went to the clinic with my mother in an ox cart. My labour was very painful, but I didn't get any injuries. When we came back with the baby, I didn't know how to take care of her, so my mother taught me. She helps me a lot, even at night when my baby cries.

I don't like being a mother, but I like my child. I feel good when I look at her. I worry about her future and who will take care of her. When she grows up, I'll take her to school so she gets educated because it's good for her. I'll also warn her and tell her not to go out with boys.

Before I had the baby, I was in seventh grade and I really liked school. My favourite subject was math and I wanted to become a doctor. I hope I can go back to school when the baby is six months old because then my mother can take care of her. I want to become a nurse, and I know that if I study and pass the exam, I can do it.

I've recently learned you can protect yourself from getting pregnant. You can go to the clinic and get contraceptives, but I'm too shy to go there and ask for it. I've stopped sleeping with boys.

MULENGA'S MOTHER MARY'S ACCOUNT:

I was very sad when I learned about Mulenga's pregnancy. When it was time for her to give birth, I went with her to the clinic. I was scared because I know what it's like. I felt like it was me going through everything again. The first weeks Mulenga wasn't very caring, so I took care of the baby and taught her how to do it. I hope she can go back to school, when the baby gets older. She's not allowed to have any more boyfriends.

I had no idea how you get pregnant. I didn't even know I was pregnant. We didn't learn about those things at school.

Mulenga 14 years old

IT IS GOD'S WILL WHETHER YOU HAVE CHILDREN

MUNA (14), MOTHER OF RIM, THREE MONTHS OLD, JORDAN

Muna lives with her daughter and her husband in a refugee camp in Jordan due to the war in her home country Syria. Her pregnancy and delivery went well, without complications. Muna wants to have more children and doesn't want to go back to school to finish her education.

MUNA'S STORY

I live in the camp with my husband and his parents. My parents and my brothers are here, too. I used to go to school both here and in my home country Syria. I liked school, but I stopped. I have a daughter now, so I can't go.

I was 13 when I first got pregnant. I was happy, except that I felt sick the last few months. I gave birth to my child in the camp clinic and I was in pain for about two weeks afterwards.

Every morning, I get up around seven or eight to breastfeed my daughter. Then I do the household chores. I get a lot of help taking care of my daughter from my in-laws and my husband.

My daughter Rim is fine but she throws up a lot. I think she's losing weight because of all the vomiting and diarrhea. She's had it for two months. I talked to the doctor, but he said it's normal.

It's a big responsibility, but I'm glad I became a mother. I'd like to have three more children. I don't want to continue my education. I don't know if it's difficult to get contraception here because I've never asked for it. There are women who get pregnant even if they use contraception. If God wants to give me children, it will happen whether I use contraception or not.

There are women who get pregnant even if they use contraception. If God wants to give me children, it will happen whether I use contraception or not.

Muna 14 years old

CHAPTER 5
NO ONE SHOULD DIE GIVING LIFE

Girls who get pregnant within two years of their first period – or who are not yet fully developed – are at greater risk of experiencing complications during pregnancy and childbirth. They may also take longer to recognise signs of complications and seek proper care. If they are unmarried, they might delay seeking help because they fear that they will be met with judgmental attitudes.

This is why very young girls in low- and middle-income countries have twice the risk of maternal morbidity and mortality than older girls and women. However, with prenatal care and safe delivery, this heightened risk can be eliminated.

The younger the mother, the greater the risk to the baby. In low- and middle-income countries, babies born to mothers under 20 years of age have a 50 per cent higher risk of being stillborn or dying in the first few weeks, than infants born by mothers aged 20-29. Every year, about one million children born to adolescent mothers do not make it to their first birthday.

Inadequate access to basic health services and essential medicines leads to poor women dying from causes that could have been prevented or treated.

HRH Crown Princess Mary

I WAS SAVED AT THE LAST MINUTE

KEYA (14), MOTHER OF RAHIM, TWO MONTHS OLD, BANGLADESH

Keya lives with her husband, her son and her in-laws in an urban slum area in Bangladesh. Keya and her husband fell in love and wanted to get married against their parents' wishes when she was 13 years old. Due to excessive blood loss, Keya almost lost her life during the delivery. She was saved by emergency blood transfusions at the hospital and has now recovered.

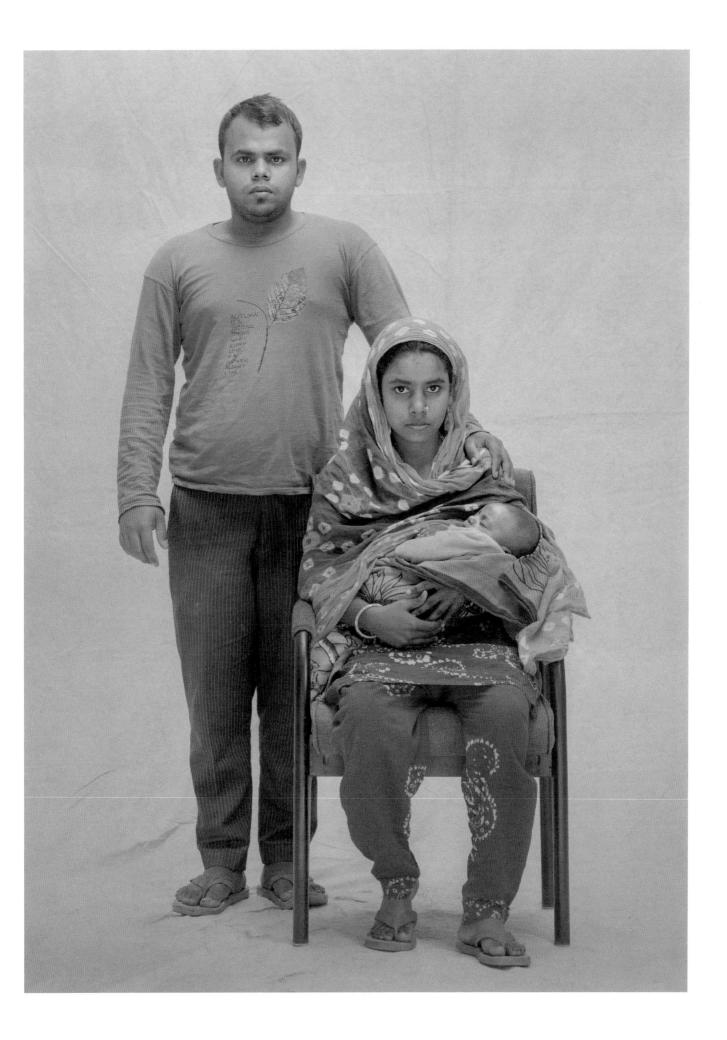

KEYA'S STORY

When I got married at 13 I was happy. I only went to school for one year because my family was so poor. I had spent several years at home helping my mother with the household chores.

I got to know my husband from our neighbourhood and knew I wanted to marry him. I was glad when I got pregnant two months later. I wanted to have a child. When I first felt the labour pains, I didn't tell anyone. My mother-in-law asked me if I was feeling sick and I said I was. She tried her best to deliver my baby for me but she couldn't do it by herself.

Then my mother came and took me to the local clinic. I delivered a baby boy at the clinic but afterwards my placenta didn't come out so I lost a lot of blood. I felt so bad and my face went white. That's when they sent me by ambulance to the hospital, where I got seven blood transfusions. I stayed in the hospital for a week and started to feel better.

I like being a mother but it's difficult to do the household chores, since I have to look after Rahim at the same time. I knew how to take care of a baby from before because I have a younger brother who is two years old. I've learned everything from my mother. She also helps me take care of Rahim. I'm in touch with the local clinic and I take him there to get vaccinations and nutritional advice.

I don't want any more children now; maybe later when Rahim grows up. I didn't know anything before about how to get pregnant or the risks of being a young mother. Now I've learned about family planning from the doctors at the clinic, and I'm going to start taking contraceptives soon.

I think a lot about Rahim's future. We don't have enough money. My husband works as a painter but right now he's out of work. It's sometimes hard to provide food and clothes for our family. I worry that I won't be able to give my son a good education. I want to find work so I can help him go to school and become a lawyer. Let's see what work I can get.

My placenta didn't come out so I lost a lot of blood. They sent me by ambulance to the hospital, where I got seven blood transfusions. I didn't know anything about the risks of being a young mother.

Keya 14 years old

I don't know what I want to do in the future. I want to first finish my education and then find a job. When I have enough money, I would like to have a family. I'd like to one day go back to Port-au-Prince, where I lived before our house was destroyed in the earthquake. I've been in this camp for five years now and don't know how long I'll stay.

In the future, I'll make sure to protect myself. My sister works at the health clinic nearby and says she'll help me get contraception if I need it. They say once you've had a baby, you can get injections or pills, but if you haven't been pregnant they will give you condoms. I don't have a boyfriend right now so I don't need that.

He was so small. They put him in an incubator and they would call me every day so I could go and see him. Then, after six days, he died. They told me he was too small and that he couldn't breathe well.

Elianne 15 years old

ELIANNE'S STORY

I was seven months pregnant when I felt a pain in my lower belly. After a week, I decided to have a check-up to see what was wrong. But each place I went to refused me and told me to go somewhere else. They said my condition was very serious and that the baby or I could die during delivery.

When I finally arrived at the hospital, my sister and I spent several days outside because they wouldn't let us in. I was really suffering there on the street. When they realized I started to have big contractions, they took me inside. They gave me medicine and after lots of pushing, my baby boy finally came out. He was so small. They put him in an incubator and they would call me every day so I could go and see him. I was so tired. Then, after six days, he died. They told me he was too small and that he couldn't breathe well.

We didn't have a funeral. The hospital didn't even give his body to me. The day he died, I was the only one at the hospital so afterwards I went home and my family took care of me.

I don't feel anything. I'm not sad, though. I didn't want to have a baby. When I discovered I was pregnant, I was sad. I knew my parents wouldn't send me to school anymore. And I also realized I wasn't mature enough to have a baby.

I met my boyfriend near my home, in a park. He came over to me and we started talking. Not long after, we fell in love and he became my boyfriend. We spent a lot of time together.

When my parents found out about my pregnancy, my father chased me out of the house and threatened to hit me. My parents were not happy. They suggested I should get an abortion but I didn't want to. Later I agreed to take a pill but it didn't work. Neither did the herbal treatments with leaves that they got me to drink. Nothing worked.

I don't know what I want to do in the future. I want to first finish my education and then find a job. When I have enough money, I would like to have a family. I'd like to one day go back to Port-au-Prince, where I lived before our house was destroyed in the earthquake. I've been in this camp for five years now and don't know how long I'll stay.

In the future, I'll make sure to protect myself. My sister works at the health clinic nearby and says she'll help me get contraception if I need it. They say once you've had a baby, you can get injections or pills, but if you haven't been pregnant they will give you condoms. I don't have a boyfriend right now so I don't need that.

He was so small. They put him in an incubator and they would call me every day so I could go and see him. Then, after six days, he died. They told me he was too small and that he couldn't breathe well.

Elianne 15 years old

CHAPTER 6
DEPRIVED OF ALL DIGNITY

G irls who are too physically immature to go through child-birth are at particular risk of experiencing complications during delivery – including having a prolonged, obstructed labour. If the girl does not have access to getting a C-section in time, the birth may leave her with obstetric fistula.

Obstetric fistula is a hole between the vagina and the bladder and/or rectum, which causes urine and/or stool to leak uncontrollably from the vagina. The hole is caused by the pressure of the unborn baby against the pelvis. This pressure prevents the flow of blood to the internal tissue, which then withers and leaves a hole. Due to the prolonged delivery, the baby will often be stillborn.

Girls and women living with fistula smell and find themselves excluded from their community and their school; many of them end up being left by their husbands. Often, girls and women with fistula live alone in the most remote huts in the village – in isolation and shame.

With access to proper care and C-sections, fistula can be prevented. And most fistulas can be repaired through surgery. However, such a procedure is only performed by specialised surgeons – and women and girls living with fistula have very limited access to such treatment as they are typically among the poorest in the community.

I have met women who had undergone fistula surgery. The hope in these women's eyes was testimony to the unbearable suffering they've endured and how they dreamt of returning to the lives they once knew.

HRH Crown Princess Mary

I HAVE TO GET PREGNANT AGAIN

ANITA (15), BANGLADESH

Anita lives with her husband and her in-laws in a rural village in the Northern part of Bangladesh. She was forced to marry when she was 13 years old and got pregnant at 14. Her delivery was very difficult and when Anita was finally taken to a hospital after two days, her son was dead and she had been badly injured. Now she is waiting for an operation.

ANITA'S STORY

I feel so sad. My baby died in labour and I'm still in such pain; I can't walk properly. I was in the hospital for 12 days after giving birth because of my injuries. Since my delivery, I have had no control over urinating. Lying down in bed, I don't leak. But as soon as I get up and take a step, I urinate. I wet my clothes and everything. I worry if I'll ever get well. I'm praying that God takes care of me. I had a son, who died. God took him away. Please give me a chance to be a mother again. Without children, a person's world is so dark.

Before I got married, I lived with my mother, father, seven sisters and a little brother. My family is poor so I went to school for only two years. One day my aunt came to visit and asked my father about marrying me off. I wasn't happy. I didn't even know the man, I was going to marry.

After five months of marriage, I got pregnant. I was happy to be expecting a child and my husband was happy too. I didn't know about the risks of pregnancy being as young as I was. I hardly talked to anyone; I just stayed at home.

My delivery was very difficult. It was ten o'clock at night when my water broke. The village Daayi (a traditional midwife) came but she couldn't get my baby to come out. Then they took me to the local health facility but they couldn't help me, either. So they transferred me to the town hospital. After nearly 28 hours of labour, I was in so much pain. Even the baby's hair was pulled out as they forced the delivery, but still it was impossible. Finally, they delivered my baby but he'd already died.

I was sent home with a catheter, so I had to come back and change it every ten days. But I wasn't getting any better. So one day I broke down and cried and that's when my neighbour asked what's wrong with me. I shared my story with her and she told me that I could get treated for my condition. Then my husband brought me here, to the Fistula Rehabilitation Centre.

Now, I'm waiting for an operation. After my surgery, I want to learn how to tailor so I can make some money. But I also need to get pregnant again. My husband's still with me but he's not very supportive about my injuries. He blames me and asks me why I have this condition when other women don't. This is why I need to recover. If I don't have another child, my husband will leave me. Who will take care of me then? I pray that I will recover completely.

My delivery was very difficult. I was in so much pain and my baby died. Since my delivery, I have had no control over urinating. I wet my clothes and everything.

Anita 15 years old

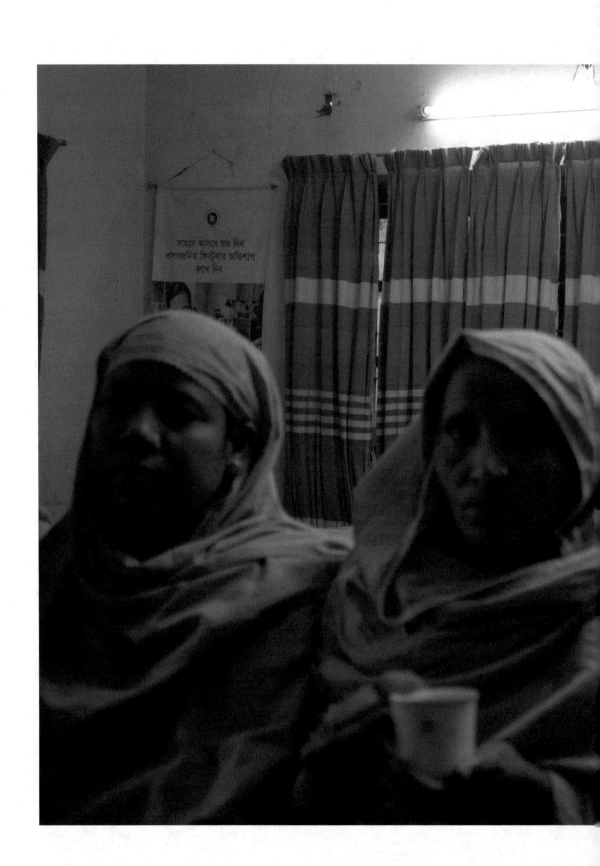

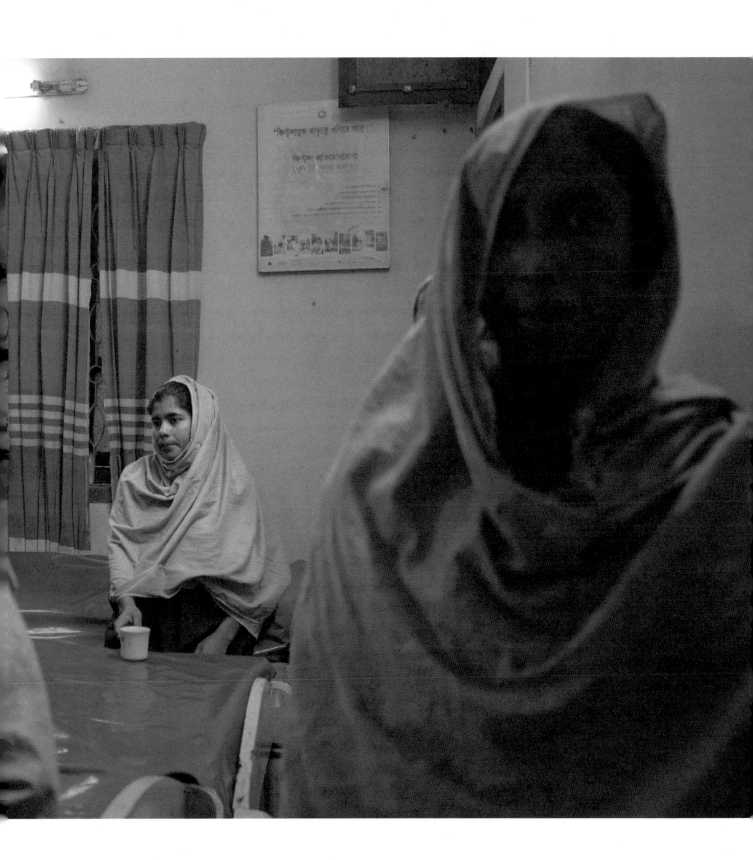

CHAPTER 7
A HARD-HITTING REALITY

Research shows that incidences of involuntary sex are more frequent among young adolescents than among older girls and women. In fact, young age is considered a risk factor when it comes to the likelihood of being subjected to violence by an intimate partner.

Gender-based violence related to schooling is a global problem, and it takes many forms. For example, assault on the way to school, or forced sexual activity in exchange for good grades.

Globally, it is estimated that one in every three women will be subjected to violence or abuse – most often by someone she knows. A study of 133 countries found that one in five women has been sexually abused as a child.

Unfortunately, gender-based violence is often perceived as something women are not only exposed to, but also share responsibility for – and for this reason, they should just accept it. Deep-rooted ideas about masculinity often play a major role when it comes to the prevalence of gender-based violence. Girls and women face more violence in places where social norms embrace male toughness, dominance, and control of girls and women.

Girls and women who are subjected to violence typically have no access to legal support or to services that may support their safety, health and well-being.

Men and boys are part of
the solution. I have spoken
with men who had previously
been violent offenders against
women. Now they work to
change the attitudes of other
men in their communities.

HRH Crown Princess Mary

RAPE CHANGED MY LIFE

AÏSSA (15), MOTHER OF FATI, 13 MONTHS OLD,
BURKINA FASO

Aïssa lives with her daughter, her mother and her two
sisters in a rural area in Burkina Faso. She was sexually
abused by her teacher when she was 14 and got
pregnant as a result. The teacher was later suspended
for one year.

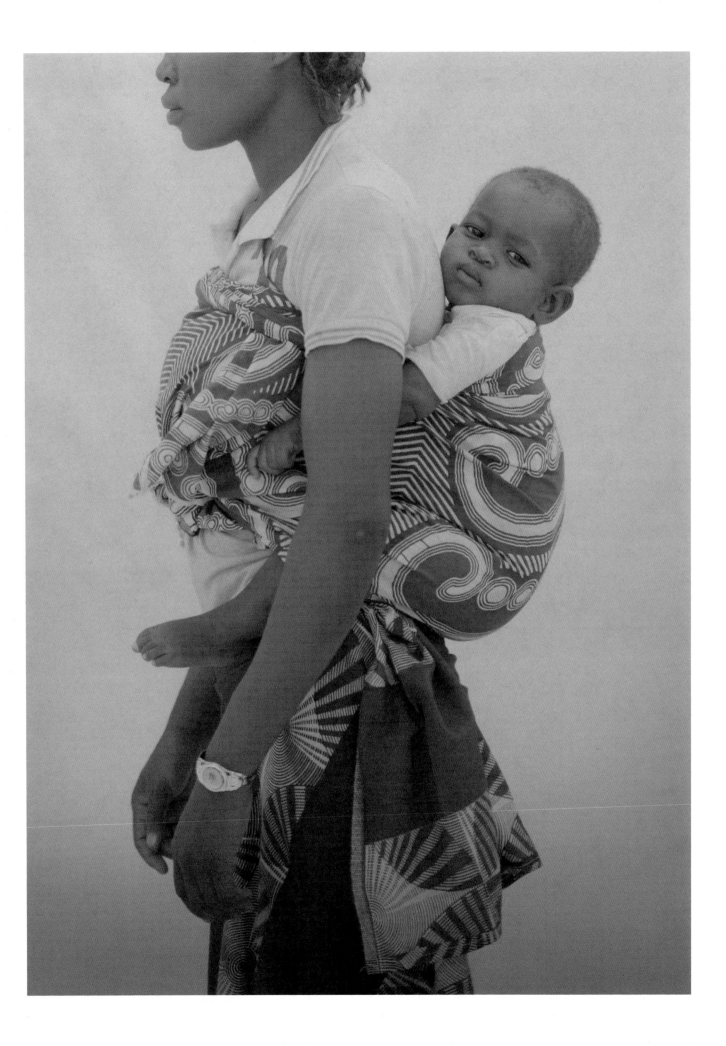

AÏSSA'S STORY

I was 14 when I got pregnant. It was after my primary school exam. When I had taken the exam, I called my teacher to find out about my results. Then he had my number. He kept calling and asked me to come and see him. I said I wouldn't go. Then one day, he threatened me and said that if I didn't come, I would have a problem. So I got frightened and went there to get the results of my exam. Then he raped me.

Last time I saw him was outside the local police station after my parents realized I was pregnant. My parents and his parents agreed that his family should take care of me until the delivery. So I was living with them for five months, until I had the baby. My teacher never came by while I was there. When I was in his parents' house, they paid for my school fees but that was all. They never gave me a cent, never gave me any clothing, nothing, but the mother took me to antenatal consultations.

Before I got pregnant, my father provided me with everything I needed and paid for my school fees. But after the baby, he stopped and isn't giving me anything anymore. He doesn't even want to see me. He doesn't care about me. Now I live with my mother, my daughter and my two younger sisters. I've stopped going to school. My mother is very supportive. Whenever I need something I can't afford myself, she tries to help me.

When I wake up in the morning, I bath the baby. Then I make some pancakes, which I try to sell during the day. I don't really make a good profit out of them but I need to work. When I'm finished, I come back home to my mother. She has a small plot by the riverside where she grows some vegetables. I go there to help her do some farming and I come back in the evening. I carry my baby with me everywhere.

I'm not really feeling happy as a mother. Motherhood to me is really painful because when my child is sick, when she has fever, then it's my responsibility.

Before the baby, I went to school. Now, when I see my friends going to school, it makes me sad. Very sad. I wanted to be a mother later – not now.

When I had taken the exam, I called my teacher to find out about my results. Then he had my number. He kept calling and asked me to come and see him. I said I wouldn't go. Then one day, he threatened me and said that if I didn't come, I would have a problem. So I got frightened and went there to get the results of my exam. Then he raped me.

Aïssa 15 years old

VIOLENCE IS QUITE COMMON

LUMILENE (15), MOTHER OF CLAIRINA, SIX MONTHS OLD, HAITI

Lumilene lives with her daughter and her parents in a camp for internally displaced people. The family has lived there since the earthquake hit Haiti in 2010. Their house was destroyed and their economic situation is very difficult. There are many young mothers in the camp and violence against girls and women is common.

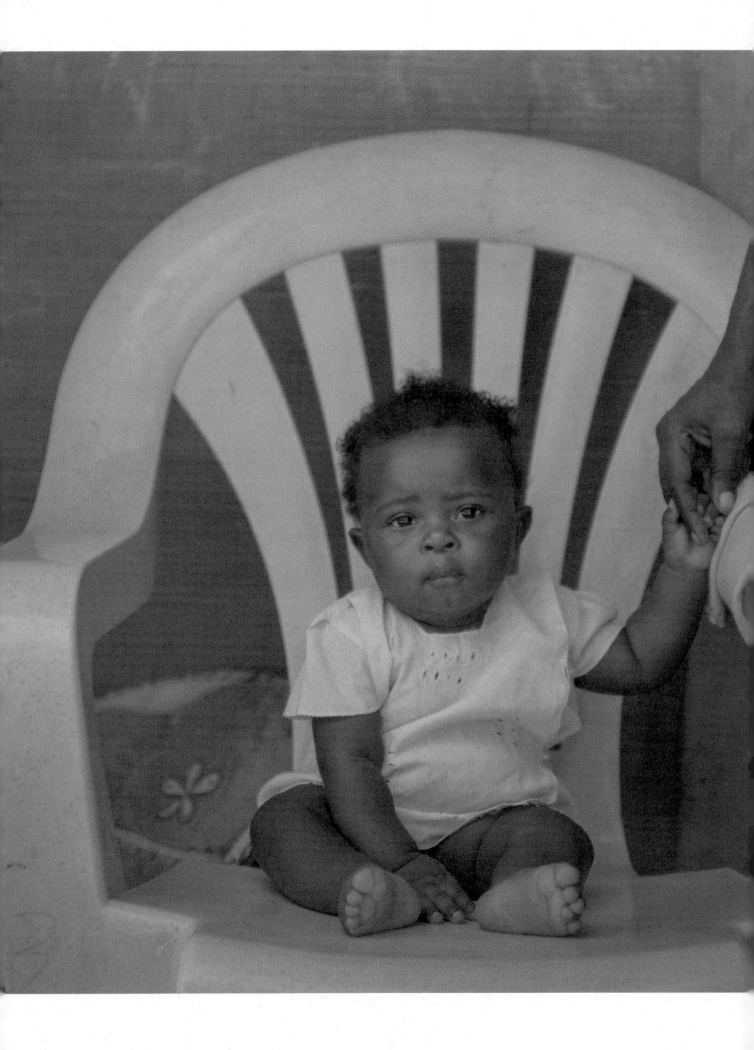

LUMILENE'S STORY

Since the earthquake, I have lived in a camp with my parents and little sister. Our house was destroyed and now we've lived here for five years. My mum sells bread but sometimes she doesn't have enough money.

I'm not the only one in school who is a mother. You know, young girls here, their parents are very poor. I'm told some of the girls trade sex for money and food. Violence is quite common. I have friends who've been abused by men. You shouldn't fool around with these men and never become their friend. Once you're their friend, they can do whatever they want to you. It's hard for a girl to say no.

I met a boy who became my boyfriend. He is 24 years old and lives nearby but he is not my boyfriend anymore. I was 14 when I discovered I was pregnant. I wanted to get rid of the baby but my mum didn't agree. She wasn't angry; she just thought I should keep the child. For four months, I was sick and I threw up all the time. I had to stop going to school.

When it was time for the delivery, my mum took me to the hospital. I wasn't afraid although I was in a lot of pain. After more than 24 hours in labour, I finally gave birth. The hospital didn't give me any pain relief. They just used scissors and made a cut. It took time for me to heal. I was lying in bed, I couldn't walk and my whole body ached. But when I saw my baby girl for the first time, I was so happy; I'm happy to be Clairinas mother.

It's easier now that Clairina's six months old. When she was just born, I couldn't go out and my mother had to tell me how to hold her. I'm back in school, in the eighth grade. I wake up early, cook porridge and I breastfeed her before leaving her with my mother. When I come from school, I go and fetch water, prepare food, do the laundry and other household chores. When I need to do my homework my mum takes care of her. Right now, Clairina is a bit sick. She's got a bad cold, coughs a lot and she has eye troubles, too. I had an appointment with the doctor but I never went. I didn't have money for the transport.

I'd like to get married in the future. I would also like to work as a nurse but it is difficult because my parents don't have any money to pay for my education. So now I'm thinking that I'd like for Clairina to become a nurse instead. She can live out my dream.

Since the earthquake, I have lived in a camp with my parents and little sister. Our house was destroyed and now we've lived here for five years. Violence is quite common. I have friends who've been abused by men.

Lumilene 15 years old

I DON'T WANT IT TO HAPPEN TO ME

MONDE (15), MOTHER OF RAYMOND, TWO MONTHS OLD, ZAMBIA

Monde lives with her son, her parents and her siblings in a very remote area in Zambia. She got pregnant at the age of 14 with her boyfriend and finds it difficult to be a young mother.

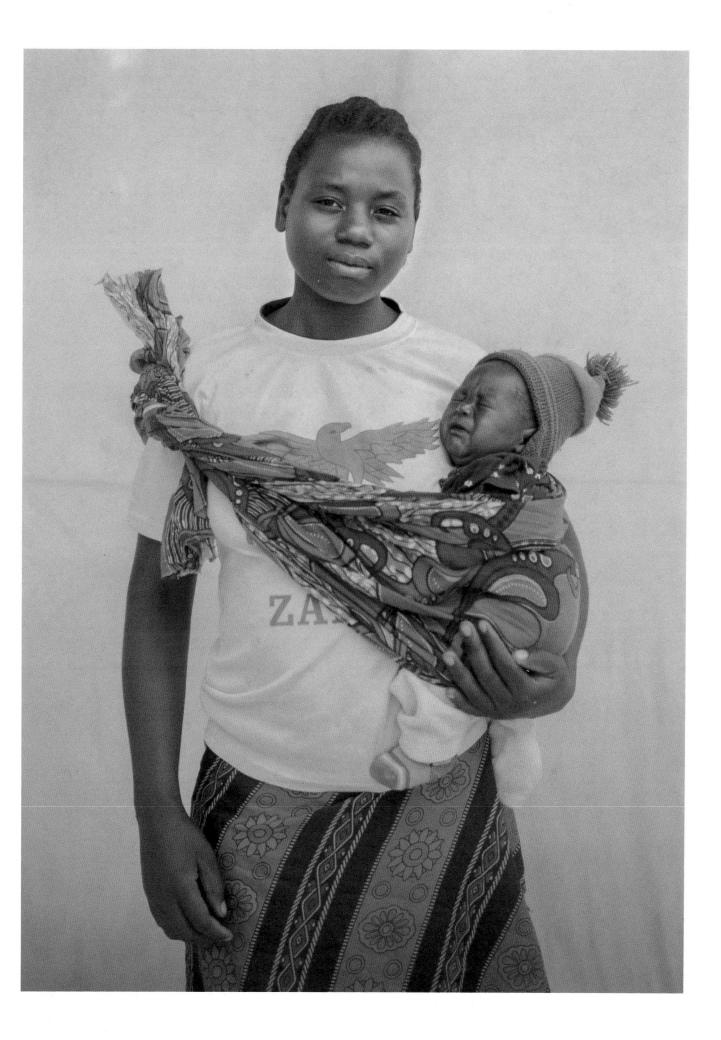

MONDE'S STORY

When I told my mother about my pregnancy, she was annoyed and got mad at me. She asked me who the father was and I told her it was my boyfriend who lived nearby. We don't intend to marry, it's only friendship. My parents called my boyfriend and his parents. He denied he was the father but I insisted and said he was responsible for the pregnancy. My parents believed me but didn't force me to marry him.

In school, we learned about periods and pregnancy. I knew at least how you became pregnant but I didn't think it would happen to me. It's easy for young people to get contraceptives at the local clinic but I didn't go there because, well, I was shy. After having my baby, I wanted to start using the injectable contraceptive, but I haven't started yet.

During my pregnancy, I was still going to school. My friends laughed at me so that was annoying sometimes. There are other girls in school who are pregnant too.

When it was time for me to deliver, the father of my baby took care that I was driven to the clinic. When I got there, I threw up and then gave birth just two hours later. I wasn't afraid. I stayed strong during the whole delivery.

I don't like being a mother because I am still young. Babies cry a lot and usually get sick. The only thing I enjoy is breastfeeding. I didn't have any idea how to take care of a baby. I learned at the clinic and also got help from my mother and sister.

I miss school and would love to go back again. I will start as soon as my mother finds money to pay for it. She will look after Raymond so I can go to school. In the future, I want to be a teacher but I don't want to get married. To me it seems that women who get married, suffer. Men often abuse their wives and beat them. I don't want that to happen to me.

In the future, I want to be a teacher but I don't want to get married. To me it seems that women who get married, suffer.

Monde 15 years old

Men often abuse their wives and beat them. I don't want that to happen to me.

Monde 15 years old

CHAPTER 8
GIRLS ON THE RUN

Humanitarian emergencies put young girls at an increased risk of unwanted pregnancy, sexually transmitted infections (including HIV), maternal death and illness. Moreover, the risk of sexual and gender-based violence – including rape and forced marriages – also increases.

In emergency situations or humanitarian crises, there is often no or limited access to health care, including contraception, prenatal care or midwifery.

When access to limited services is cut off, young expectant mothers will not receive the care they need during pregnancy and childbirth. And they will typically not be able to provide adequate care for themselves and their new-born baby.

Humanitarian crises undermine the lives of everyone but, for pregnant women the situation is even more acute.

HRH Crown Princess Mary

LIFE IN THE CAMP IS TOUGH

AMIRA (15), MOTHER OF SAMER, ONE YEAR OLD, AND AMAL, 12 DAYS OLD, JORDAN

Amira lives with her husband and their two children in a refugee camp in Jordan. She had to stop attending school because of the war in her country. Both her children were born at the maternity clinic in the camp. At the clinic, advice is also provided on health, contraception and about taking care of children. But life in the camp is tough and monotonous.

AMIRA'S STORY

It's so hard to take care of a child when you're a child yourself. For example, I'm not sure if I should be carrying my children all the time. Plus, I have to take care of my husband too. I don't have any free time for myself. My children take up much more time than all the household chores. My new-born baby cries a lot. Sometimes, I don't know why he's crying. He just does.

When I first got pregnant, I felt tired but I was happy, too. I thought I'd have a baby who would entertain me and fill up my free time. Now with two children, I don't get any rest at all.

My husband and I had some problems in the beginning. But after I gave birth to my first child, he started to help me and understand me more.

My body isn't the same as it was before. I often feel tired. No matter what I do, my body feels so weak and powerless. My family who lives nearby helps with my eldest son, but not with my youngest.

Thank God, my children are doing fine. They can get sick but it's normal because they get well again. My eldest son does so many funny things. I like to play with him because then I feel like a child, too. When we play, I feel like he's my friend, not my child.

I studied in primary school. I left school only because of the situation in my home country Syria. I want to study again in the future. I'd like to be a teacher. I don't want any more children now. It's enough. I have two and I should take care of them. I want to use contraception in the future. It's easy to get but I didn't know this before. I want to give my children all the things I wasn't able to have. For example: toys, a house and an education. I really want them to have a comfortable life.

For a long time, I've felt the need to speak about things that weigh on me. But I have no one to talk to. I feel alone here. There are things I can't change, like living in this camp. Life is hard here. Nothing's normal. You don't visit anyone and no one visits you. You just take care of your children and your husband all the time. That's it.

For a long time, I've felt the need to speak about things that weigh on me. But I have no one to talk to. I feel alone here. Life is hard in the camp. Nothing's normal.

Amira 15 years old

HRH The Crown Princess is the photographer behind this photo of Pieter ten Hoopen who is showing Kiswendsida his shots of her. Burkina Faso, 2016.

ABOUT #CHILDMOTHERS

#childmothers is a photo exhibition, a website and now a publication.

With #childmothers, Plan International and UNFPA, the United Nations Population Fund, seek to give 17 girls and mothers a voice, and draw attention to the reality they share with far too many young girls around the world.

Photographer, Pieter ten Hoopen and journalist, Sofia Klemming Nordenskiöld have met the child mothers portrayed in this book in five countries across three continents: Bangladesh, Burkina Faso, Haiti, Jordan and Zambia.

It's the country offices and local partners of UNFPA and Plan International that have identified the young mothers who are part of #childmothers. Some of them take part in programmes that support very young

mothers and their children. The ethical guidelines of both organisations have been observed throughout the project. The girls and their families have given their consent to the girls' participation. All names have been changed, and we do not give exact information as to where the girls live.

Plan International and UNFPA would like to thank everyone who have contributed to #childmothers. First and foremost the child mothers themselves, who have shared their personal stories with us. We would also like to extend our appreciation to our partner organisations and to Danida and Sida for their financial support.

To learn more about early motherhood, go to www.childmothers.org. The site also features short videos with the 17 girls from this book.

The large piece of fabric travelled the world with photographer Pieter ten Hoopen to serve as background to recreate the classic family photo, which has inspired #childmothers. Zambia, 2015.

ABOUT UNFPA

UNFPA, the United Nations Population Fund, is the lead UN agency delivering a world where every pregnancy is wanted, every childbirth is safe, and every young person's potential is fulfilled. UNFPA works in more than a 150 countries to advance sexual and reproductive health and rights. UNFPA partners with governments, civil society, the private sector and academia and adopts a human rights-based approach in its work. UNFPA focuses on women and young people – also when engaging in humanitarian response efforts.
Visit: www.unfpa.org

ABOUT PLAN INTERNATIONAL

Plan International is an independent global child rights organisation working to make positive and lasting changes in the lives of children and young people. Plan International works in more than 50 countries across Africa, Asia and the Americas. The organisation supports children and their communities to acquire the skills, knowledge and confidence they need to claim their rights. Most of Plan International's country offices have programmes focusing on adolescent sexual and reproductive health and rights.
Visit: www.plan-international.org

HRH The Crown Princess is a keen photographer, who often brings her camera when travelling as in this photo from Mozambique, 2012. Two not previously published photos taken by The Crown Princess feature in this book.

HRH CROWN PRINCESS MARY

UNFPA Patron

As Her Royal Highness The Crown Princess mentions in the introduction to this book, her participation in a Mother's Day event in 2009 served to spur her engagement in advancing sexual and reproductive health and rights for women, men and young people. In 2010, this engagement translated into The Crown Princess becoming patron of UNFPA, the United Nations Population Fund.

HRH The Crown Princess is an exceptional advocate for women and girls; whether she addresses world leaders in UN-fora, talks to 100,000 people from the stage of the Global Citizen concert in Central Park in New York, talks about access to contraceptives with young people in Mozambique or plays games on human rights with 10-year old pupils at a school in rural Denmark.

During her travels for UNFPA, The Crown Princess brings hope to the women and young girls she meets; she does so with a genuine interest, a professional insight, and a profound empathy: meeting them as a fellow human being, as a woman, and as a mother.

UNFPA wishes to thank The Crown Princess for her contributions to this book; contributions which lend a voice to the girls and women of the world. This is deeply appreciated by UNFPA; it makes a positive difference to our work. Our gratefulness to The Crown Princess encompasses her entire engagement as patron of UNFPA.

PHOTO REFERENCES

COVER:

Front cover; Photographer: Pieter ten Hoopen, photos from #childmothers

Back cover; Photographer: Torkil Adsersen, Scanpix. Mozambique, 2012

Page 7; Photographer: Clement Bihoun, UNFPA, Burkina Faso

Page 8 left; Photographer: Antti Kaartinen, UNFPA Nordic Office

Page 8 right; Photographer: Torkil Adsersen, Scanpix

Page 9; Photographer: Franne Voigt

Page 10; Photographer: Hanne Juul, Billed-Bladet

Page 12; Photographer: Théo Somda/Dimanche Yaméogo, UNFPA, Burkina Faso

Page 13; Photographer: HRH Crown Princess Mary

Page 15; Photographer: Keld Navntoft, Scanpix

Page 19-163; Photographer: Pieter ten Hoopen, photos from #childmothers:

Page 19, 20-21 and 26-27; *Kiswendsida (15) with her daughter Koudbi, one month old, Burkina Faso*

Page 24-25; *Kiswendsida with her grandmother and Koudbi, Burkina Faso*

Page 29; *Rabeya (16) with her husband Jalal (30) and their daughter Kushum, three years old, Bangladesh*

Page 32-33 and 35; *Rabeya with Kushum, Bangladesh*

Page 37; *Angelica (13) with her son Lucner, three months old, Haiti*

Page 40-41; *Port au Prince, Haiti*

Page 43; *Zainab (15) with her son Bilal, two years old, and daughter Karima, eight months old, Jordan*

Page 44-45; *Street in Jordan*

Page 49; *Taonga (15) with her daughter Margaret, four months old, Zambia*

Page 50-51 and 55; *Taonga fethcing water, Zambia*

Page 58-59; *Street in Bangladesh*

Page 61, 62-63 and 66-67; *Nargis (15) with her son Nayeem, one and a half years old, Bangladesh*

Page 69; *Thandiwe (15) with her husband Jonathan (19) and their daugher Anna, nine months old, Zambia*

Page 72-73; *Thandiwe with Anna, Zambia*

Page 76-77; *Horse stable, Burkina Faso*

Page 79 and 80; *Poko (15) with her son Tiga, three years old, Burkina Faso*

Page 87; *Oxcart, Zambia*

Page 89 and 92-93; *Mulenga (14) with her daughter Felicity, five weeks old, Zambia*

Page 94; *Mulenga doing the dishes, Zambia*

Page 97; *Muna (14) with her daughter Rim, three months old, Jordan*

Page 100-101; *Amman, Jordan*

Page 105; *Rabeya with Kushum*

Page 107 and 110-111; *Keya (14) with her husband Jangir (21) and their son Rahim, two months old, Bangladesh*

Page 113, 118-119; *Elianne (15), Haiti*

Page 116-117; *Refugee camp, Haiti*

Page 123 and 125; *Anita (15) Bangladesh*

Page 128-129; *Anita with other women at the fistula rehabilitation centre, Bangladesh*

Page 133; *Country side, Zambia*

Page 135 and 136-137; *Aïssa (15) with her daughter Fati, 13 months old, Burkina Faso*

Page 141 and 142-143; *Lumilene (15) with her daughter Clairina, six months old, Haiti*

Page 149; *Monde (15) with her son Raymond, two months old, Zambia*

Page 153; *Monde with girlfriends, Zambia*

Page 156-157; Photographer: Sima Diab, UNFPA, *Zaatari refugee camp, Jordan*

Page 159; *Amira (15) and her husband Ahmad (24) with their children Amer, one year old, and Amal, 12 days old, Jordan*

Page 162-163; *Amira in the refugee camp*

Page 164; Photographer: HRH Crown Princess Mary

Page 165; Photographer: Sofia Klemming Nordenskjöld, Plan International Sweden

Page 166; Photographer: Franne Voigt

#CHILDMOTHERS
First edition
ISBN: 978-87-93085-02-2

Editor: UNFPA Nordic Office
Author, the stories of the girls: Plan International Sweden

Layout and cover: LenePerez.dk
Typography: UNFPA and Eureka

Repro: Satsbutikken
Printed in Lithuania 2017 by Balto Print

Published by:
UNFPA, 2017
www.unfpa.org

With support from the
"Danida Information Grant".